MOOSE! Tracks
(Dedications)

I would like to thank the following individuals —
without their support, love and encouragement,
Choose the MOOSE! would not have been possible:

Monica J. Elchlepp — For being my visionary partner
and for her unending love, support, understanding
and encouragement.

Employees Everywhere — The MOOSE! Philosophy
was established to assist businesses and their employees in a cultural transformation. After witnessing first
hand the substandard way businesses interact with
and treat employees, I have created a manual of trans-
formational hope for you. This book focuses on what
a business can do, both internally and externally, to
create a workplace where a positive creative atmos-
phere abounds.

Choose the MOOSE!

An Outrageous way for <u>ANY</u> Organization to Thrive through its Employees

Peter A. Cicero, SPHR, MBA
Cicero Endeavors, Inc.

First published by Dog Ear Publishing
4010 W. 86th Street, Ste H
Indianapolis, IN 46268
www.dogearpublishing.net

ISBN: 1-59858-143-0

This book is printed on acid-free paper.

Printed in the United States of America

Like a shot ringing through the air on a crisp day, Sidney's alarm clock rang jolting her out of a nice, warm, comfy slumber. Sidney opened one eye and peered at the clock. No, it wasn't the mistake she was hoping for, it was six o'clock and, yes……..it was Monday.

As she struggled to open both eyes and get her tired body out of bed, she grew increasingly irritated at the thought of going into work. "I don't want to go to work!" she yelled out, hoping someone would answer. But, alas, no one did and Sidney was faced with the bitter reality of pulling herself out of bed and going back to a job where she did not want to be.

Dreaded feelings of work soon transformed into piercing thoughts of what the week would bring. She was growing impatient with doing stories that no longer seemed to grab the public's attention.

Sidney was a journalist. It was something she dreamed of being since she was a little girl. As she continued to get ready for work, she reminisced of her younger years and how exciting it was to read fun magazine articles, it didn't matter if it was fashion, wildlife or current world events. It was the article itself and how it was written that most grabbed her attention. And since then all she's ever wanted to do was write stories that made people take a step back and think.

Sidney thought to herself, "Maybe this morning wasn't so bad. My shower successfully washed my grumpy mood down the drain. Breakfast helped too. Listening to the news on the local radio station driving into work reminded me of the fact that there are others worse off than I. At least I have a job. At any rate, it has turned out a little better than it started. I'm ready to take on the day."

Well, those thoughts were dashed the moment she walked through the door of *InFokus Magazine.* Her heart sank as she heard the president of the company hollering at an employee for missing an early morning deadline. Sidney shared a quiet "hello" with the receptionist and made her way to her office.

She passed the regular gossipers — the employees pouring their coffee who stand around talking for most of the morning which they count as work — and those who have the same look she woke up with that morning. A look that spoke all of her same thoughts — "this is the last place I want to be right now."

At their morning staff meeting, the editorial director, William Beaumont, was discussing what stories needed to be covered for the week and to whom they were assigned.

As Sidney listened to William rattle off assignments, she couldn't help but wonder if it was like this at other companies. The monotony from week to week, negative attitudes throughout every department to go along with management who just doesn't seem to have the energy and visionary focus they once possessed. Editorials were flat and lacked the spark necessary to keep the public coming back for the next edition of *InFokus*. All of this combined with profits at the lowest in the magazine's fifteen year history left anxious employees feeling nervous about their jobs.

Sidney wasn't sure how *InFokus* got to this place, but she was well aware that if something didn't change, quickly, she too would be feeling uneasy about her job and the future of the company. After all, she just joined *InFokus* two years ago and wasn't ready to make a change in her career. Not yet anyway.

The sound of her name broke the deep thoughts she was having and she immediately began concentrating on William. Sidney sat intently listening to the details of her assignment.

William said, "Sidney, this is a unique story, and I want you to cover it. It's about a company called CatchAway Manufacturing, Inc., that is crediting a moose to its current level of success. It caught my attention when I happened to hear about them at the Chamber of Commerce meeting the other night, and I'd like you to check it out.

Lord knows our company could use a boost in
readership. If it's that different, people will read
it, at least for curiosity sake."

"Great. Thanks William," she thought. "I
get to write about a moose — I don't know
anything about a moose — what was he thinking?
Then again, he gave ME the assignment which
means he trusts me to deliver it in a professional,
yet provocative manner. Cool!"

Sidney had exactly one month to complete the story and prepare it for publication. She immediately set to work and began researching CatchAway. She wasn't terribly excited about the story, but she was determined to approach it with an open mind and positive attitude.

As she researched, she discovered CatchAway was once a less than profitable fishing lure and tackle manufacturer. Only five years earlier, earnings were in the red; stocks were dangerously low; employee retention was suffering at a loss of 85%; and morale was at an all time low.

As a result, the company took action and significantly turned over its senior management team in a bold effort to begin generating profits.

However, it was the steps they took to accomplish all this that Sidney found most astonishing. The more she read, the more anxious she grew to speak with the president, Arthur McKenzie.

Sidney's meeting was set for 9:00am sharp. As she pulled into the driveway to the building, she noticed a huge bull moose carved out of wood. She began thinking of the impact the moose has had on this company. Her stomach ached with nerves. This could be the most unique story she's ever covered! She arrived at 8:45 and was politely greeted by the receptionist at the front desk.

"Hello! My name is Sidney Wagner. I have a meeting with Mr. McKenzie at 9:00."

"Good morning Sidney. He's expecting you. Please have a seat and I'll let him know you've arrived," the receptionist said with a smile.

Mr. McKenzie himself came to the lobby to collect Sidney for their meeting. He was a tall, imposing man. He stood 6'5" and was built like a lumberjack, yet possessed the manners of a polished and refined man.

"Good morning. I'm Arthur McKenzie." he said in a deep voice, smiling.

"Good morning Mr. McKenzie. I'm Sidney Wagner. Thank you very much for taking the time to meet with me this morning."

"Please, call me Arthur." he replied.

As they made their way to his office, they passed a series of uniquely decorated offices. Sidney noticed several different styles of décor and wondered what the company's policy was on interior decorating. Nowhere had she ever seen such a great display of personality and expression. It was tasteful and classy but also comfortable and welcoming.

Arthur's office was modestly decorated with family pictures on the desk and stacks of projects scattered about. It had several windows which allowed the sunshine to warm the creamy taupe colored walls. His office was relaxing and not stuffy like she'd originally envisioned the president's .

Arthur was obviously an outdoorsman. There were several mounted fish and a fox on his walls. But, as Sidney scanned the room, she came across the largest mount she had ever seen. On the wall behind Arthur's desk hung the mounted head of a bull moose! Sidney couldn't believe her eyes. What is the story behind that moose?

"Have a seat, Sidney," said Arthur. "Where would you like to begin?"

When *InFokus* originally contacted him,

Arthur was flattered to be asked to interview for a major magazine regarding the accomplishments of his company and the progress they've made.

"I'm very interested to know what the significance is behind the moose, which is prominently displayed, in one form or another, throughout your company," Sidney replied.

"Well, it all began with a hunting trip I took six years ago. I was fortunate enough to have the opportunity to do a hunt in Alaska. A friend of mine mentioned how much he enjoyed the pristine environment and talked about the overall picturesque and tranquil beauty, not to mention the size and abundance of trophy game in that area. He invited me to accompany him on another hunting trip he was taking, this time for moose, and I couldn't refuse.

"I had never seen a moose in real life and was

very excited at the thought of it. The trip would last seven days total. It took us one day's travel to get to Alaska and another hour by bush flight before we finally arrived at our camp. Upon our arrival, we were cheerfully greeted by locals who welcomed us 'cheechakos' (newcomers to Alaska) into their tent for a warm meal and drink. This was a family owned establishment and offered a true Alaskan experience.

"The next morning we left early by horseback to begin our hunt. It wouldn't be until the trip's third day that I happened upon one of the greatest experiences of my life. Up to that point, I had the privilege of watching black bear fish for food in the streams, plenty of elk grazing in the open land and several smaller creatures scampering about, but no sign of a moose. And then it finally happened.

"On day three, in the late afternoon, one very

large and majestic moose wandered in a fair distance from my tree stand. I raised my rifle, and as I looked through the scope with a heartbeat that seemed to rock my entire body, I took what I planned to be the fatal shot. With a sweaty finger, I squeezed the trigger and took the shot. The bull moose was enormous and collapsed to the ground with all its weight. I quickly got down from my stand and began to walk to where I felled the moose.

"Darkness was fast approaching and as I made my way to the spot where the moose should have been, there were only remnants of blood. I tracked it as far as I could until I was out of daylight. I returned first thing the next morning and resumed my search where I left off the night before. After about forty-five minutes, I found him lying down, looking so peaceful. I couldn't believe his tremendous size! I had only viewed him through my rifle scope but to see him close up was an exciting moment. I reached down and touched his face and much to my horror, his eyes opened!

"Startled, he sprang to his feet. By this time, my heart was beating harder than it ever had before, and I couldn't feel my legs. I wasn't sure if I was on MY feet! There I was staring up at a moose who was staring down at me. I could feel his hot breath on my face."

Sidney's eyes were fixated on Arthur and her hands were perspiring as she listened intently to his story as he continued.

"I read about how aggressive moose can be when they are in a defensive mode. Moose lick their lips, put their ears down and the hair on their neck and back stand up as a warning. A

moose that decides someone has invaded its
'personal space' will knock down the offender
and kick and stomp until the threat stops moving.
They have powerful front legs, and I frankly was
waiting for a fatal kick to the ground.

"In the moment my life flashed before me, he
turned and ran off, leaving me shaking and ready
to pass out. I collected myself, sort of, and
continued to search for my moose. The one I
stumbled upon was not injured but just sleeping,
since there was no blood to be found. I continued
searching and saw another moose lying on the
ground.

"Scared of another close call, I grabbed a light
tree branch and tossed it onto the moose's belly.
It did not move. This was my moose from the day
before.

"That story will always remain fresh in my

mind. What hangs on my wall is a constant reminder of that humbling experience. It changed my life and the entire future of this company," Arthur said with a proud look on his face.

"In what way?" Sidney asked.

"After my Alaskan moose hunting experience," Arthur began, "I became very intrigued with this animal and started to do a lot of research. The moose has been around in one form or another for more than a million years. It knows that in order to properly grow and survive within its environment, it must change and adapt.

"For instance, the moose's food sources change with the seasons. In the summer, the moose enjoys munching on aquatic plants and the occasional leaf off a tree—consuming 50-60 pounds of aquatic plants per day. However, in the winter, they flatten down snow to reach the grasses below, they feed on tree bark and stems in willow flats and coniferous forests, but always balance their needs with nature so they don't damage the plants.

"By natural instinct, the moose is resourceful, using only what is necessary to survive, keeping balance and harmony within its own habitat. The moose understands its size and strength and uses these characteristics to build and protect rather than break down and destroy. In their 'defending circles,' each moose knows where it fits and what its role is within the circle. Within the moose's own defending circle, it is aware of its member's needs and what it must do outside of that circle to protect and assist others."

"It already sounds like mankind could stand to take some lessons from the creatures of the wild," Sidney stated with a very interested expression on her face.

Arthur continued, "Knowing what to do in the harsh and wild environment is the difference between life and death. The moose continue to exist by setting examples and teaching the ways of survival to those within and around the defending circle. During migratory efforts, young moose are taught how to search for food and where to go as the seasons change. How the moose behaves and copes with the challenges of today will have an affect on the generations of tomorrow.

"This is a majestic animal, one of the largest in nature, and although many view the moose as clumsy due to its enormous size and weight, it actually is quite agile and graceful. Its speed and strong defenses allow for quick escape from danger. The moose is commander of the territory it occupies and although the threat of prey by bears, wolves or even man will always be present, it goes to great extremes to defend itself and others in order to maintain its survival."

At that moment, there was a knock on Arthur's door. "Come in," he said.

"I'm sorry for interrupting," Alex said with a smile.

Alexandra Heyworth, better known as Alex, was Arthur's executive assistant. She was quick witted and took great pleasure in doing her job with a flair of humor. She had a colorful personality and always found a way to make people laugh. Her responses to Arthur and the rest of her colleagues often times left them walking away scratching their heads because they were unable to match her response with one just as quick. She had a play on words for everything.

On a more professional side, CatchAway couldn't ask for a more dedicated and energetic employee who takes her job and responsibilities very seriously.

"Arthur, you have an overseas call on line two that desperately needs your attention," said Alex.

With that, Arthur said to Sidney, "I'm going to have to take this but, if you have time, there are some other members of the company I'd like you to speak with until we are able to chat some more."

"Oh, I definitely have time and would appreciate that opportunity," Sidney said.

"Alex, could you please arrange meetings between Sidney and Ricci and possibly Brian if there's time yet this morning?" Arthur said as he was walking Sidney out of his office.

"It would be helpful to hear what others have to say besides me. I'll look forward to speaking with you again soon," Arthur said with a big smile.

"Thank you very much for your time, Arthur. I'll be back in touch in a week or so," Sidney said.

He shook her hand and returned to his office to take his call.

Sidney chatted with Alex while waiting for Ricci to arrive. She was pleasantly surprised when she saw her approaching the two of them. Ricci stood five feet, seven inches tall. She was an attractive woman with a beautiful figure who obviously took a lot of pride in herself. Her clothes were well coordinated and in style with the current fashion. She carried herself with grace and confidence. Her head held high, she greeted everyone with a smile and a warm "hello." However, hidden underneath all her grace and charm were some powerful weapons. She was a tough woman who always let people know where they stood with her. There was no guess work. She was honest and worked hard to build up her credibility with the employees through out the company. She was very demanding and her expectations of herself and of others was very high.

"Good morning Alex!" Ricci said with a smile.

"Hey! Good morning Ricci! How's everything going?" Alex asked.

Ricci answered, "We're in good shape and slightly ahead of schedule with some of our orders!"

"That's a switch over last week." Alex said.

"That's for sure!" responded Ricci. "Well, hello! You must be Sidney!"

"Yes. That's right," began Sidney. "I'm a journalist from *InFokus Magazine*. I'm here to do an article on the Moose and how it's influenced your company."

"It's a pleasure to meet you Sidney! I'm Ricci,

the Plant Manager here at CatchAway. Why
don't we take a walk down to my office? We'll
chat for a bit and then if your schedule will allow,
I'd like to invite you to an employee
communications meeting."

"Ricci," said Alex, "I have Sidney scheduled
to meet with Brian in his office two hours from
now. He wants you to ring him if that doesn't
work well for you."

"Thanks Alex!" said Ricci.

"I'd be happy to attend the meeting, and I
appreciate the invitation to let me in on some of
the day to day things," said Sidney. "I
understand CatchAway has gone through
significant changes over the years. I would like to
hear what your role has been and how you have
progressed from where you were then to where
you are now.

"Arthur has given me information about how he has been inspired by the moose and examples of what he's learned from his research. However, we didn't get to discuss how all this relates to the business and the impact it's had on CatchAway specifically."

They arrived at Ricci's office which was conveniently located near the plant floor. Like Arthur's office, and the others Sidney noticed, hers was decorated to suit her personal taste.

"I feel like I'm in Italy!" said Sidney.

"Well, I've been able to go a few times over the past four years and completely fell in love with the country. This is my way of bringing some of that here for others to enjoy as well. I make sure I visit a different region each time I go, and I always concentrate on absorbing as much of the local culture as possible for a true Italian experience," answered Ricci.

She incorporated a Mediterranean theme to capture the essence of the calmness of the old world. Her walls were a creamy colored Venetian style plaster with a coffee wash top coat. In her office were several paintings depicting scenes from Venice, Tuscany and Rome, among others. Tropical floor plants and statues on pillars completed the setting. It was like a brief escape to Italy — tranquil and inviting.

"Do you have anything like this at *InFokus*?" asked Ricci.

"No," Sidney said in a disappointing tone. "We are actually in a bit of a tough situation, morale wise, and I can't imagine anyone wanting to take the time at this point to make their surroundings enjoyable. Our employees could use a bit of a boost. To my knowledge, no one's ever even expressed a desire to have anything of the sort."

Sidney quickly caught herself losing her positive disposition and regained focus on Ricci. "Anyway, enough of that. Please, talk with me about you and CatchAway."

"Well, let's see. Let me begin about six years ago. That was a time of great personal struggle. I felt like I needed a team of wild horses to drag me into work each morning. I didn't want to come here, and once I got here I didn't want to be here. The old regime had a top-down mentality. There was only one way of doing things — theirs. They did not want to listen to anything anyone had to say," Ricci explained.

Sidney was shocked as she listened to Ricci, at the similarities of the old CatchAway and what she was currently experiencing at *InFokus*.

Ricci continued, "Distrust, rumors, and gossip were rampant. Everyone was always waiting for a bomb to drop."

Sidney was amazed at how open and honest Ricci was about the former culture. She was anxious to hear what role Ricci played in all of this.

"How did this sit with you?" Sidney asked hesitantly.

"It certainly wasn't something I signed up for and I put up with it because I felt I had to. Plant management jobs were scarce in this area. I couldn't just leave. I had a family to support."

Sidney couldn't help but pick up on the sour taste that experience had left with Ricci. She could see the passion in Ricci's eyes as she reflected back on a less than pleasurable moment in her career with CatchAway. Ironically, Ricci had painted a picture very similar to what Sidney was currently experiencing at *InFokus*.

"What role did the senior members of the staff play, and how did that affect you?" asked Sidney.

"I really can't speak for what the senior staff members were doing. With the exception of Tony, our senior sales guy, it was evident that they didn't have a vested interest in the direction of the company. The perception was that they were only concerned about two things: themselves and whether they were going to make their bonus. When Arthur came on board, the first major change he made was to revamp the top management team, with the exception of Tony," answered Ricci.

"What did you think of that bold move and how did that ultimately affect you?" Sidney asked.

"It was a welcome change," began Ricci. "Prior to that, I was doing whatever I could to hold my team together. It became more and more difficult to keep making it seem like the president and the rest of his team's ideas were driving results. Looking back now, I've come to realize that the procedures we were told to implement were only to satisfy the stockholders of the company and weren't really put in place to be effective. It looked good on paper, but the company was quickly becoming a money pit. Orders were missed due to inefficient production procedures and a lack of data accuracy within the computer system we had at that time. It also didn't help that the senior staff was fudging numbers to make bonus and ultimately hold onto their positions. They didn't care what was going

on through out the company and it showed,"
Ricci explained.

Ricci's tone was bitter. With her ethical and
professional mannerisms, it was clear this was
extremely frustrating for her to witness and not
have any control over.

"I don't mean to come off sounding bitter or
have you interpret my remarks of our former
management staff as disparaging. That's not the
case at all. Arthur was bluntly open and honest
with the rest of us about the damage that had
been done and the rough road ahead to correct
it.

"It's just frustrating to see things like this take
place right underneath your nose and know
there's not a darn thing you can do about it.
Arthur coming in was like a breath of fresh air.
He introduced us to the MOOSE Philosophy and

things really took off," said Ricci with a sigh. "It wasn't an overnight transformation, but we didn't waste any time turning the company around — one piece at a time. Arthur reminded us that change needs to be embraced by everyone in order for the company to be successful." she explained.

"Talk to me about the moose and how it's impacted CatchAway." Sidney said.

"We were introduced to the MOOSE a few days after Arthur started at CatchAway," began Ricci. "It didn't take me long to realize that this man and his MOOSE were exactly what CatchAway needed. At the time, most of our employees didn't understand or weren't aware of what was going on within the company. The hourly employees on the floor were treated like pieces of equipment. No one was permitted to think for themselves. We didn't pay people well and there was significant talk of a union coming in.

"When Arthur came in, one of the first things he did was hold a plant meeting. In this meeting, he assured everyone that things were going to change. He let people know their ideas were welcomed and would be listened to. To be a MOOSE organization, the mechanisms must be in place to allow for a superior flow of knowledge within the organization. Everyone involved must know how the company is performing. What are the company's goals and objectives? Where is the company going?

"This philosophy must flow down from the top and be supported at all levels. No one person should hold all of the information for the organization. A MOOSE organization should be a

free information environment where employees
are empowered to make decisions because they
have the knowledge of where the organization is
heading. To be a MOOSE organization, a
business needs to be ready to share what it takes
to survive!"

"Wow! What a concept!" blurted Sidney.

"Yes it is. Are you ready to see it in action?
It's almost time for the meeting," said Ricci.

"Great! I'm looking forward to it," Sidney
said with excitement.

Sidney put on safety glasses and headed to
the floor. She was observing Ricci interacting
with the employees. She was definitely in tune
with the plant floor. It was obvious she had a
genuine care and concern for all the employees,
and they appreciated her interest as well. As they
rounded the corner by the paint department, Ricci

stopped. "See all of these charts and graphs on this board?" she said pointing to a large corkboard easel in the paint department. "It's one of the ways we support the MOOSE on the floor.

"Before we were in the dark about our progress, or lack thereof, and the overall status of things. Now, with the MOOSE, each line or cell has a responsibility of achieving the numbers explained by the graphs. The graphs show how each cell is performing on a daily basis. In other words, they keep track of their own efficiency rates. Each line or cell is responsible for setting its own rate, knowing the performance of the line, and determining the corrections if the rates are not being met.

"Every employee knows where we as a company stand because of our superior knowledge transfer. We operate under a 'no surprises' policy."

The two women soon came to a medium size conference room where employees were gathering. The room quieted down when they saw Ricci. Sidney took a seat in the back to observe as Ricci began to speak.

"Good morning everyone! Welcome to our monthly SOB meeting."

The room chuckled with laughter.

Ricci continued, "Let me begin this morning by introducing our guest. Sidney Wagner, sitting in the back of the room, is a journalist from *InFokus Magazine*. She's here to do an article on our company and the MOOSE. It seems we've been discovered! I've invited her to our meeting to give her a glimpse of what a MOOSE organization is all about."

The entire room turned around to look at her

and although she was slightly embarrassed at being singled out, she felt warmly welcomed.

"Let's start with an update of the numbers."

Ricci then proceeded to tell the employees of the new developments in sales, marketing, customer service, and new product development. Sidney was pleased to see many of the employees taking notes and asking pointed questions. It was nothing like the meetings she experienced at *InFokus* where the managers would talk while the employees just stared into space. After a series of marketing questions, Ricci said, "Well, enough from me. Let's hear how each department is performing."

Sidney watched as an employee from every department went to the front of the room and gave an operational performance update. When finished, the presenting employee was asked various questions from Ricci and the rest of the audience. This routine continued until all departments were heard from.

At the close of the meeting, Ricci reminded everyone that they were the business and nobody knew more about the business than they did. She encouraged them to keep tracking their progress and reiterated that she was there to support them.

The room filled with applause as all the employees congratulated each other on a job well done. Ricci caught up with Sidney after the meeting.

"I see we only have a few minutes before your meeting with Brian. Can I answer any additional questions for you?" Ricci asked flushed with excitement.

"Wow!" said Sidney. "That was great.

Everyone seemed to be on the same page and knew what needed to be done. Everyone seemed to feel important."

"Not seemed," interrupted Ricci. "Each employee IS important to CatchAway. Our employees understand the business and work to make it thrive."

Sydney continued, "It was such an upbeat meeting. Why did you give it such a negative name? What does it mean?"

Ricci laughed. "You mean SOB?"

"Yes," Sidney said with a nervous laugh.

Ricci explained, "It's a reflection on the past. The way things used to be. The acronym really means State of the Business. But, it also serves as a sober reminder that we could all too easily slip back to the way things used to be. It is everyone's responsibility to keep us moving forward."

The women continued walking and talking and soon found themselves back in the office area.

"It's about time to get you to Brian Whittaker. You'll enjoy him. He is our customer service manager and a lot of fun to be around." Ricci said.

They continued down the hall and arrived at Brian's office.

"It's been a pleasure sharing my experiences with CatchAway's progression and the whole MOOSE Philosophy with you Sidney. Here's my card. Don't hesitate to contact me if you need additional information. I'd be happy to answer any of your questions," Ricci said as she extended her hand with a smile.

Sidney was full of so many different thoughts with Arthur's input, and now Ricci's, that she found herself energized and not exhausted like she typically was after a morning packed full of meetings.

"I truly enjoyed talking with you about the company and your challenges with CatchAway. You're a strong woman and I admire your accomplishments. Thank you so much for your time Ricci," Sidney said.

I t was obvious Brian's passion was golf. His clubs were propped in a corner and his office walls were covered with several plaques and pictures of beautiful golf courses from around the world. He played on a pro tour at one point and held several championship titles. However, his focus eventually turned toward raising a family. He made the decision to withdraw from the professional golf scene and utilize his expertise to coach young up and coming golfers. He now coaches 8- to 13-year old kids on summer weekends.

Ricci did the introductions.

"Brian, this is Sidney Wagner. She is here from *InFokus Magazine* to do a story on the MOOSE and how it's impacted CatchAway. I

need to be getting back on the floor. Take care
Sidney."

"Well, good morning Sidney! I'm Brian
Whittaker. I manage our Customer Service
Department. Come in and take a seat," Brian said
with a hand shake and a smile.

"It's a pleasure to meet you Brian!" Sidney
said. "I cannot get over the personality of each of
your offices. How many years have you been
golfing?"

Brian thought for a second and then replied,
"Oh, gosh. I guess it's been about 26 years now.
Eight of which were spent golfing professionally."

"How was it making the transition from the
professional golf circuit to the business world,
specifically to a manufacturing company?" Sidney
asked.

"Not hard at all," began Brian. "I met Arthur at a golf outing several years ago. I was paired up with him. The pace of play was extremely slow so we had a lot of time to talk. Arthur took the time, on that golf course, to tell me about the MOOSE Philosophy. I was stunned. This concept sounded so simple and so easy to follow that even a golf pro could do it."

Sidney laughed.

Brian continued. "I then took the opportunity to tell Arthur about my service golf philosophy."

"Your service golf philosophy?" Sidney asked.

Brain smiled. "Yes. That was the philosophy I was using on the tour, but it hadn't always been my philosophy. Originally I was a one man show and didn't need anyone. Well, it showed — missed cuts, poor finishes. I figured there had to be a better way. So, I took a couple weeks off and began to study the other players.

"It soon became apparent to me that golf was not just about me playing. It was about my team. How the team was performing; how the team was there as a service. I stopped focusing on me and started to focus on we. "

"I am sorry Brian," interrupted Sidney. "But I don't see how you can think of golf as a service."

Brian laughed. "Most people don't see golf as service. They see it as something that is totally focused on the individual golfer. But, my golf *was* a service. I was there for a bigger goal then myself. I was there for the audience. I was there for my caddie. I was there for my agent, fans, sponsor, and the list could go on and on. This is exactly what I told Arthur that day on the course, and he was just as stunned as I was. We amazed each other with how similar our philosophies were. A couple of years later, Arthur called me and asked me if I was interested in making a career change. I was getting tired of always being on the road, and I could not pass up the opportunity of working with the MOOSE Philosophy. Arthur and I spent a lot of time together incorporating my service philosophy into the MOOSE. The rest is history!" Brian said waving his arms around his office pointing to the various customer service awards.

Sidney liked Brian. He was cute and had a great demeanor. Sidney felt Brian would be a great guy to deal with.

Sidney asked, "So where does customer service fit in the MOOSE Philosophy?"

"We are obsessed with providing our customers and consumers with outrageous customer service," responded Brian. "Our customers need to be satisfied 100% of the time, and they need to want to come back for more. None of our customers will experience better customer service anywhere else — period!" responded Brian.

"That's a pretty lofty goal, isn't it?" asked Sidney.

"It has to be," answered Brian. "If we don't, then are competitors will. There is always someone waiting to take your place. That's why we use Outrageous as our term. It makes us forward thinking — proactive instead of reactive to our customer's needs. We need to go above and beyond what our customers expect (want) and deliver what they really need — a truly incredible outrageous experience; something they can't get anywhere else. We are all here to serve others and to make each and every interaction with CatchAway a truly memorable one!"

Sidney observed Brian. He was just beaming. It was obvious that he was incredibly passionate about serving others. Just by listening to him, Sidney began to question her personal outlook on life. She was just thinking of how she could serve others better in her own life when Brian asked her a question.

"So what do you think Sidney?" Sidney felt embarrassed that Brian had caught her daydreaming. She blushed. "I think that you're great. Oh, I mean it's great."

Sidney was turning redder by the second. "It's a great philosophy, but does it work?"

"Does it work?" Brian blurted with a chuckle. "C'mon, I'll show you."

In addition to all the customer service awards

in Brian's office, he took her into the customer service department. "This is our wall of fame." began Brian.

Sidney was amazed. The wall was filled with letters and emails from customers telling about the great products and outrageous service they received from CatchAway.

Brian continued, "Likewise, over here, we have our wall of shame. This is the wall where we did not live up to an outrageous experience." Sidney looked at this wall. There were a few letters on it. "What do you do with these?" Sidney asked.

Brian smiled. "We try to move them over to the wall of fame. We learn from the shame responses and put procedures in place so it doesn't happen again. We do not want the same issue coming up more than once. The first time an issue arises, it is an opportunity. The second time the same issue arises, it is a problem. If we are unable to move a customer from shame to fame, then they receive a phone call from Arthur.

"Arthur has even gone to visit some of our customers just to make sure that they were completely enamored with our product. At CatchAway we don't just want a satisfied customer; we want an enamored customer who has never experienced anything like us. That is what Outrageous customer service is all about."

They continued walking through the customer service department. Sidney had never seen a customer service department like this. Here, all of the employees seemed to be actually listening to the customers. They asked probing questions to try to determine the actual issue the customer was experiencing. Most of all, they did it with a smile on their face. Sidney commented on this to Brian. "I haven't seen one of the representatives not smiling," she said with amazement.

Brian responded, "We want all of our customers to have a smile come through the phone to them. It makes our customers feel better to know that we care enough to treat them to the very best service."

The two soon finished their tour and found themselves back in Brian's office.

Brian asked with a twinkle in his eye, "Is there anything else I can help you with this morning?"

Sidney laughed. "Spoken like a true customer service professional, Brian."

"No problem at all," Brian said. "If you have anymore questions just give me a ring."

Sidney could feel the pangs in her stomach and was looking forward to lunch. She was thrilled to have captured so much information in just one visit and felt optimistic about meeting the deadline for this assignment. As she drove back to the office, she began to wonder what it would take to turn *InFokus* into a dynamic and outstanding performance organization like CatchAway.

This assignment had already done a lot to boost her enthusiasm about wanting to come to work every day. She quickly recognized attitude has everything to do with performance. A great attitude equals optimal performance potential. There was no reason *InFokus* had to continue down the path it was on. The company was staring self-destruction in the face and no one had stepped up to change it; let alone recognize it.

As Sidney thought about the morning's interviews, her anxiety grew on how to convey this information properly to the rest of the business world. She knew she had a very unique story on her hands, and if she could get this excited after one morning of discussions, she imagined how others would feel after reading her article.

She pulled into the *InFokus* parking lot and quickly dropped off her things at her desk. She ran into one of her co-workers and they decided to go to lunch together. As they walked to a diner a block down the street, they chatted about their mornings and the assignments they were currently working on.

Sidney was all too quickly reminded of the

morale of the people at *InFokus* in speaking with
her colleague over lunch. Conversation included
everything from complaining about work to the
person in the adjacent cubicle to eventually how
down in the dumps her co-worker was about her
situation at home.

Sidney's mind was reeling as she listened to
her friend ramble one negative sentence after
another. And then it dawned on her at that
moment. She sat and wondered how happy
people really were with themselves. Her mother
always told her, "You need to love yourself before
you can begin to love anyone else." Is that what
this was all about? If we aren't content with
ourselves, how can we begin to reflect a positive
attitude toward anything else? Was Mom right all
these years?

Sidney had yet to meet with Tony Morino in sales at CatchAway, and she was going to approach Arthur about perhaps meeting with Alex, his executive assistant, as well. She felt that with those two interviews, she would have a well rounded opinion of the organization's status today and the outlook for the future. With Tony and Ricci having the lengthiest tenure with CatchAway, they would provide the valuable glimpse to the past and how the company pulled itself out of the negative position it once held. The only thing left would be a final meeting with Arthur and she could wrap things up.

The next day, Sidney rang Tony for an available time to meet. He was out of town on business but would be back in a week. Not a

problem. This would give her a good chunk of
time to pull together some detailed notes and get
her thoughts organized. She also spoke with
Arthur, and he was more than willing to have her
interview Alex.

Interview Notes
Moose Project
CatchAway Manufacturing Company, Inc.

Arthur: **What a moose does in its environment**

1. The moose has been around in one form or another for more than a million years. It knows that in order to properly grow and survive within its environment, it must change and adapt.

2. The moose is resourceful, using only what is necessary to survive, keeping balance and harmony within its own habitat.

3. The moose understands its size and strength and uses its characteristics to build and protect rather than break down and destroy.

4. In the "defending circle," each moose knows where it fits and what its role is within the circle.

5. Within the moose's own defending circle, it is aware of the other members' needs and what it must to do outside of that circle to protect and assist others.

6. The moose is a majestic animal, one of the largest in nature, and although we might imagine a moose as clumsy due to its enormous size and weight, it is agile and graceful.

7. The moose is a commander of the territory it occupies.

Ricci: Communication

1. People must know their ideas are welcomed and will be listened to.

2. Mechanisms must be in place to allow for a superior flow of knowledge within the organization.

3. Organizations should be a free information environment where employees are empowered to make decisions based on the knowledge of where the organization is heading.

4. A business needs to be ready to share with its employees what it takes for the organization to survive.

5. Operate under a "no surprises" policy.

6. Employees are the business and nobody knows more about the business than they do!

Brian: Customer Service

1. Stop focusing on me and start focusing on we.

2. Need to be obsessed with providing our customers and consumers with outrageous customer service.

3. Customers need to be satisfied 100% of the time, and they need to want to come back for more.

4. None of our customers will experience better customer service anywhere else—period.

5. Need to go above and beyond what our customers expect (want) and deliver what they really need—a truly incredible outrageous experience; something they can't get anywhere else.

6. We are all here to serve others and to make each and
every interaction a truly memorable one.

7. The first time an issue arises, it is an opportunity. The
second time the same issue arises, it is a problem.

A week later.............

Tony Morino was not your stereotypical sales person. He was a mature man, sharply dressed, and well groomed; it almost looked like he just stepped off Wall Street. He enjoyed the "pretty boy" look and pulled it off well. However, behind the designer clothes and accessories was one of the most genuine, down-to-earth men you could ever meet. His roots were planted deeply in rural America, and he was as country as country gets. He drove a pick up truck complete with cowboy hat and fishing pole. An avid fisherman, it was evident he was a natural fit with CatchAway. He was the epitome of what the company stood for. His hobby was crafting flies; a skill he learned from his father as a young boy.

Growing up in a small town, he was expected to use his imagination and creativity to pass by lazy summer afternoons. He and his brothers would frequent the local creeks in search of slippery prizes to bring home to the family for dinner.

Today his passion for fishing and love of the outdoors was clear to his customers. Tony was able to sell products effortlessly and with a suave style others could only imagine having.

"Hi Sidney!" Alex said as she looked into Tony's office.

"Hello Alex! Well, I'm back, but my work here is just about finished. I am here to meet with Tony Morino. Is it OK if I wait here until he's off the phone?"

"Tony is always on the phone but he knows you're here. The front desk told me you arrived. Let me know if you need anything after your

meeting is finished. It is nice to see you again!"
Alex said with a big grin.

"Actually, if it's not going to tighten your
schedule too much, I'd love the opportunity to
speak with you after I finish up with Tony."

"Oh boy," laughed Alex. "Are you sure you
want to talk to me? I might say something that
gets us ALL into trouble!" she giggled.

"I definitely do!" I think you're just the one to
shed some light on questions I might have by time
the day's over," answered Sidney.

"Well, I'll be happy to shed some light
wherever you'd like me to!" responded Alex.

Both girls laughed until they heard Tony's
conversation drawing to an end.

As Alex walked away down the hall, Sidney
looked into Tony's office. Tony was just hanging
up when he caught sight of Sidney. He motioned

for Sidney to come in and have a seat. From the sounds of it, Tony was on the phone with his best friend.

"Super. Super. That'll be great. I'll be looking for that order tomorrow then. Give my love to Janet and the boys. Thanks, I will. OK now — bye."

Tony now turned his attention to Sidney. "Boy that guy sure is good people! He is the top VP-Buyer for one of the largest sporting goods distributors in the world, and he is honest as the day is long. You must be Sidney. I'm Tony. Tony Morino. Pleased to meet you," he said as he extended a warm hand to shake.

"Nice to meet you, Mr. Morino!" began Sidney. "I have heard a lot of things about you."

"Only the good things I hope," remarked Tony. "And please, call me Tony."

"Only the good things, Tony," laughed Sidney.

"You have been with the company from day one?" asked Sidney.

"Do I look that old, Sidney?" chimed Tony. He continued, "Yes, I have been with CatchAway since we opened our doors. I love the outdoors so much that I couldn't resist working for an outdoor company. I love this stuff. It's in my blood. Can I buy you a cup of coffee?"

"Yes please." Sidney replied.

The two made their way to the CatchAway lunchroom. From the reactions, Sidney could see that everyone loved this man. It was like Tony was running for Mayor. He was shaking hands, slapping backs, and asking people about their lives. The two finally reached the lunchroom.

Tony began, "You know Sidney, I would like to treat you to more than a cup of coffee but Mac only lets me have $5 expense money!"

Sidney laughed.

"No Sidney, I'm just joking with you. Now, what can a dumb sales guy like me help you with?" remarked Tony.

"Well Tony, since you have been here for quite some time, I would like your perspective on the transitions CatchAway has made over the years and what the moose has done for you." asked Sidney.

"Any company is going to go through growing pains over the years. However, the difference was the MOOSE Philosophy and Mac," responded Tony.

"Mac?" queried Sidney.

"You know Mac — McKenzie — Art —

whatever," Tony laughed. "It's just a name! People can call me anything, as long as it's with an order," chirped Tony.

Sidney could not help but be amused by this man. She had only known him for a few minutes but it seemed like they had been friends for years.

Tony continued, "I am just a simple farm boy, Sid, but to me, the key was knowing where I fit in the organization. Before the MOOSE, everyone was going through the motions. We had no sense of direction, no sense of ownership. Since the MOOSE, we know where we stand in the organization. We all know our roles and what is expected of us. The MOOSE has done an excellent job of helping us define the playing field or parameters for what it takes to be successful. Our people realize this and now see the ability they have to impact the organization.

"By each employee understanding, knowing, and executing his or her own role in the organization, CatchAway's forward progress is unstoppable. Not bad for a sales guy, huh?"

Sidney sat there speechless. She was mesmerized by what he had just said. It was like a lightening bolt came from the blue. Everyone needs a purpose, everyone needs a fit, she thought to herself.

"Sidney." spoke Tony. "If I am talking too slow for you or if I am using too small of words just let me know. I am used to talking to sales people!" laughed Tony.

"No, Tony. You are fine," answered Sidney with a smile. "Please continue."

"Sidney, I can compare how we operate today to a machine. All parts of this machine have a specific function and each supports the next to accomplish the end result—a finished product. The pieces work in harmony with each other and the machine runs smoothly. Before Mac and the MOOSE, we had pieces of a machine. No one knew which piece was which or how the pieces fit into the machine. With the MOOSE, all of the pieces fit and the machine functions effectively and efficiently!"

A voice cut off what Tony was saying.

"Tony Morino, line 3, Canada."

"I'm sorry Sidney but I have been expecting this phone call, and it's on a big order!" said Tony.

"No problem Tony." answered Sidney. "It has been a real pleasure meeting you."

"No kid, the pleasure has been all mine. And remember, Sid!" shouted Tony as he ran down the

hall to his office. "If a sales guy can figure this
stuff out, anyone can!"

Alex was waiting at her desk for Sidney. "How's your story on the MOOSE going?"

"It's going great," responded Sidney. "I have been extremely fascinated since I first talked with Arthur. The philosophy is great and CatchAway seems like a wonderful place to work."

"You betcha! For the last couple of years it has been a great place," pronounced Alex, stretching her arms out to indicate what a wonderful place CatchAway was to work.

Sidney could tell Alex was a person who loved life. With her extremely positive attitude and her eternal smile, Alex was the personification of a model employee. She was incredibly organized and seemed to keep everyone and everything moving in the right direction.

Sidney asked, "How long have you been with CatchAway!?"

"Me?" began Alex. "Three years. I actually started on the floor. I worked there for about 6 months."

"How did you get this position?" responded Sidney. "I'm sure it was very sought after."

"What are you saying?" retorted Alex. "Don't you think I'm qualified?" she said with a friendly sneer. "No, really. Arthur liked my attitude and my willingness to try new things. I had some college education, but I quit during my sophomore year. I didn't have any money coming in so I had to find a job. The only position available was one on the floor. I told myself it was only for a short time, and I would get back to school soon."

"If you don't mind me asking, Alex, why did

you leave college?"

"What type of interview do you think this is?" laughed Alex. "I'm just kidding. I don't mind talking about myself. I made some mistakes, and I learned from them. Back in my sophomore year of college I met this guy. We fell in love, or so I thought. One thing led to another and soon I found myself pregnant. My true love, when faced with this fact, decided that a baby wasn't in his future. He gave me a choice — the baby or him."

"Sidney, allow me to introduce you to my 4 year old daughter — Abigail."

Alex passed a picture of a beautiful curly blond haired, blue eyed girl to Sidney.

"She is quite beautiful Alex," said Sidney.

"Just like her Momma!" joked Alex.

"And the father?" questioned Sidney.

"I haven't seen or heard from him since,"
answered Alex. "It was tough going for awhile. I
quit school and moved in with my parents. But, I
pulled myself up by my bootstraps and started to
put my life in some sort of order. After Abigail
was born, I figured I better go out and get some
insurance and make some money. That's why I
landed here. Get it? Landed — at a fishing
company."

"Oh," groaned Sidney, "that was a bad one."

"I have a lot more where that came from,"
continued Alex. "The best lesson I learned from
this experience is never underestimate a person's
potential. Given the chance, anyone can
accomplish something great. I am living proof of
that. That is one of CatchAway's cornerstones.
People are our greatest assets and we should do
everything we possibly can to develop those

assets. And believe me Sidney, I have met a lot of assets in my day."

Sidney laughed. "You got me with that one."

Alex continued. "Arthur came in with the philosophy of 'making everyone great.' He instilled the belief in the organization that people's lives will improve because they are working here. Those who have been with us the longest can really see the transformation and live their lives with a new attitude and outlook. The overall belief is that we are building the people who are building the business. He calls it his 'Great Theory of Organizational Development.'"

"That's a mouthful," interjected Sidney.

"It may sound like a mouthful, but it's really quite simple," responded Alex. "Everyone in the organization strives to be the best they can be. Everything the organization stands for is about giving people an opportunity. It's all about reaching your full potential. CatchAway goes out of its way to give us those betterment opportunities."

"Alex, your story is quite inspirational," complimented Sidney. "You are a real role model for people who want to make something of themselves."

"A role model, after my life?" remarked Alex. "Honey, I don't think my life could be on a box of breakfast cereal but I try to live it to the best of my ability. Everyone should try to be the best they can possibly be. That's what it's all about. If people find inspiration in what I have been through, then great! It's my, and everyone else's, job to help others along the way. That's what it's all about and that's one of the things we do best at CatchAway."

After meeting with Alex, Sidney caught up with Arthur and spent the last bit of the day wrapping things up.

"So Sidney, tell me what you have experienced so far." As Arthur asked this, he opened up a cabinet in his office revealing a large white note board. He stood poised with marker in hand waiting for Sidney's response.

"Why don't you begin with your conversation with Alex," said Arthur.

"Well," stammered Sidney as she flipped through her notes, "in summary, Alex explained the following:"

As she spoke, Arthur wrote her words on the note board.

"Great job, Sidney! I see you listened well."

complimented Arthur. "Now, if you will please, summarize your conversation with Mr. Wit himself—Tony. By the way, he didn't call me Mac did he?" Sidney blushed. "Never mind. From your face I can tell that he did. Please continue." Arthur said with a big smile.

Again, as Sidney spoke, Arthur wrote down her words.

"I am impressed with how accurately you've interpreted things, Sidney. How about your conversation with our resident golf pro—Mr. Whittaker?" asked Arthur.

Arthur continued to write as Sidney spoke.

"I can see Brian did an outstanding job explaining our customer service philosophy to you, Sidney. What about your discussion with Ricci?" inquired Arthur.

Arthur once more went to the board to write

what Sidney was saying.

"Ricci is an outstanding individual. I respect her very much," commented Sidney. "She's obviously worked very hard to rise to her current position and thinks very highly of you and this organization. She's a very genuine woman."

"You're right. I'm honored to have her with us and will continue to expect great things from her," Arthur added.

"Now that we have the summary of your discussions, let's go back and look at each one individually."

Arthur flipped the pages back to the notes on Alex.

Alex

1. Never underestimate a person's potential.

2. Given the chance, anyone can accomplish something great.

3. People are our greatest assets, and we should do everything we possibly can to develop those assets.

4. We are building the people who are building the business.

5. Everyone in the organization strives to be the best they can be. Everything the organization stands for is about giving people an opportunity.

6. It's all about reaching your full potential.

7. It's everybody's job to help others along the way.

Arthur continued, "Given what Alex told you, how would you describe what she meant?"

Sidney studied what Arthur had on the note board. She also flipped through her notes hoping to find the right answer.

"Alex," began Sidney, "was really talking about what an organization needs to do to better its employees. From my business classes in my college days, I can remember this being categorized as organizational development."

"What a brilliant job!" blurted Arthur. "You hit that one out of the park. I would now like you to focus on one word on the board."

Arthur took his marker and underlined the following word:

Strives

"Sidney, what would you call it when a business encourages an employee, by having the proper tools and programs in place, to strive to do their best and the employee actually happily does it?" asked Arthur.

Sidney responded, "I would call that trying to motivate the employee."

"Precisely," responded Arthur with excitement. "And that is the first premise of the MOOSE! Philosophy - Motivating Organizational Development."

Arthur went to the board and wrote this over the notes on Alex.

Motivating Organizational Development

Arthur continued, "I have prepared a write-up for you on the M and what it means. Read this and let me know what you think."

Arthur handed Sidney the sheet of paper. The document read as follows:

Motivating Organizational Development

A moose knows what to do to properly grow within its environment. It knows where to look for food, where to find shelter, where to find its defending circle. It understands what it has to do to survive. The moose also knows that in order to keep thriving in its environment, it must adapt, change and anticipant what changes are coming into that environment. The moose has very little influence on the environment in which it lives, yet it learns to master its surroundings.

However, unlike the moose, in our organizations we do have the ability to influence the type of environment in which we work. We also have the ability and responsibility to try and influence how our organization grows. This is known as organizational development.
Organizational development refers to the resources an organization puts forth to aid the growth of the business and the employees of that business. A MOOSE Organization has a motivating organizational development philosophy. This means that the resources a business puts forth to better itself or its employees are:

1) Needed

2) Meaningful
3) Understood
4) Utilized

In a MOOSE organization, all four need to be present. If one of those four resources breaks down, the organizational development of the business will struggle to provide a motivating environment. A MOOSE organization strives to better itself by growing the people who will grow the business.

A moose is free to grow in its environment!

"Well," Arthur began, "what do you think?"
Sidney placed the paper on her lap and responded. "I can really see what Alex meant by the 'Great Theory of Organizational

Development.' The **M** of the MOOSE is all about the organization doing things with their employees to help them become the best that they can be."

"Great Sidney!" exclaimed Arthur. "Not only that, but, what an organization does needs to be embraced by the employees. That's where the motivating part comes in. Nobody can motivate you. Only you can motivate yourself. So if a company has a great organizational development program but no one wants to utilize it, then it is useless. Both parts need to be there—a great program to better employees and a program that employees want to utilize."

"Let's move on to the next one," Arthur said as he began flipping the white pages.

He stopped on the page that said:

Tony

1. The key is knowing where you fit in the organization.

2. Everyone needs to know their role and what is expected of them.

3. By each employee understanding, knowing, and executing their own role in the organization, forward progress is unstoppable.

4. With the MOOSE, all of the pieces fit, and the machine functions effectively and efficiently

"Sidney, looking at your notes from your discussion with Mr. Morino, how would you summarize his words?" asked Arthur.

"This one is a little tougher," began Sidney. "Let's see, if you are talking about where someone fits in the organization, then you must be talking about hierarchy. Is that right?" asked Sidney.

"I couldn't have said it better myself," laughed Arthur. "Sidney, when we talk about someone making something theirs, what would you call it?"

"Well, Arthur," began Sidney, "I guess I would call it owning."

"You are correct, my dear," beamed Arthur. "That is the second premise of the MOOSE! philosophy — Owned Hierarchy."

Arthur went to the board and wrote on the top.

Owned Hierarchy

Arthur handed Sidney another piece of paper. "For your review," he began. "Please read it, and let me know what you think." Sidney began to read the sheet.

Owned Hierarchy

Moose live and travel in groups called defending circles. All of the moose in the defending circle know where they fit or stand within that circle and where they fit among other circles. Moose are free to travel within different circles but always know where their "true" defending circle is. When trouble arises, a moose knows where it can go for comfort, safety, and protection. Moose very rarely settle disagreements by fighting. The moose rely on their dominance, power, size and majesty within the circle of moose to determine the outcome of the disagreement.

We, too, in our organizations need to know where we fit. The hierarchy or "fit" in a workplace differs greatly from organization to organization. Where we see ourselves in an organization, or where we are perceived, plays a dramatic part in our performance.

In a MOOSE organization everyone knows where everyone "fits" into the organization. Everyone also knows what role they play in the organization and what is expected of them. This is known in the MOOSE world as owned hierarchy.

To be a MOOSE organization, a business

must strive to establish a "fit" for everyone
within the organization. Employees should
feel part of a defending circle in that they
know who to turn to in times of need and
trouble. The MOOSE organization works to
build incredible teams within and across
departments. An employee, like a moose,
should feel free to roam to another circle
while still knowing and feeling that he or
she "belongs" to a group that will support
and defend if necessary.
Responsibility and reliability also are keys
to an owned hierarchy MOOSE
organization. When employees know what
is expected of them and where they "fit",
they develop autonomy and responsibility
for their functions. They also know what
others are responsible for and can rely on

them to perform their roles to the best of their ability.

A MOOSE knows where it "fits" in its defending circle!

"I can see Tony really knew what he was talking about, Arthur. This is awesome. I really think you do need to know where you fit in an organization," responded Sidney.

"You're right," began Arthur. "All employees should know where they fit in the big picture of the organization. But, remember, Sidney, the organization must help the employee understand the organizational fit. Too many times I have seen employees who think they know their role in the organization, only to find out that the company had a totally different idea. It is definitely a two-way street."

"I can see that clearly now, Arthur," commented Sidney. "This is so fascinating. Please continue."

"All right then. Let's keep this bus rolling. We have talked about the M and the first O of the MOOSE. Let's now turn our attention to your conversation with Brian."

Brian: *Customer Service*

1. *Stop focusing on me, and start focusing on we.*

2. *Need to be obsessed with providing our customers and consumers with outrageous customer service.*

3. *Customers need to be satisfied 100% of the time and they need to want to come back for more.*

4. *None of our customers will experience better customer*

service anywhere else—period.

5. Need to go above and beyond what our customers expect (want) and deliver what they really need—a truly incredible outrageous experience; something they can't get anywhere else.

6. We are all here to serve others and to make each and every interaction a truly memorable one.

7. The first time an issue arises, it is an opportunity. The second time the same issue arises, it is a problem.

"You need not say anymore Arthur," interrupted Sidney. "This one is easy. Brain gave it away himself. The third premise of the MOOSE

is **O**utrageous Customer Service. That's what the
2nd O stands for; outrageous, right?"

"Right on the mark, Sidney," said Arthur as
he wrote it on the paper.

Outrageous Customer Service

"And Arthur, I am assuming you have a
write-up for me?" asked Sidney.

"You know Sidney, at the rate you're going,
pretty soon you'll have my job." Arthur grinned
and handed Sidney another piece of paper.

Outrageous Customer Service

In its defending circle, a moose knows who
it needs to serve. A moose also knows what
it needs to do outside of its circle to

effectively serve others.

In a MOOSE organization, we must make serving others our number one priority. Service must be apparent in everything we do. A MOOSE must think of everyone as the customer and must strive to provide an outstanding experience to everyone, time and time again. This is known in the MOOSE world as Outrageous Customer Service; doing everything possible to ensure the customer's experience with you is consistently outstanding. Simply put, the service level a MOOSE organization provides is outrageous. As a member of a MOOSE organization, we must provide a level of service to our customers, both internal and external, that they have never experienced before. This repeatable

outrageous level will have all of your
customers coming back for more!
**A MOOSE knows who to serve and how
to effectively serve them!**

When Sidney was finished reading, Arthur
began talking.
"This is a pretty simple concept to explain,
but the hardest one to master. I have found
through the years that many organizations view
customer service as something you do to the
outside of the organization. I strongly believe that
effective outrageous customer service begins
within the organization in how we treat one
another.
"Every single person inside the organization
is everyone else's customer. If we try to provide
all of our customers, both internally and

externally, with an incredible amount of attention and support, then we are well on our way to outrageous customer service. We are all a brand of our organization. We need to carry that branding message to all of our customers. If an organization needs to do one thing exceptionally well, it is to outrageously serve the customer!"

"Can you guess, Sidney, what the 4th premise of the MOOSE is?" asked Arthur.

"Well" began Sidney, "I would guess it has something to do with the S and since Ricci is the only person we haven't discussed..."

"Right again, Sidney" laughed Arthur as he flipped to the Ricci page.

Ricci: **Communication**

1. People must know their ideas are welcomed and will be listened to.

2. Mechanisms must be in place to allow for a superior flow of knowledge within the organization.

3. Organizations should be a free information environment where employees are empowered to make decisions because they have the knowledge of where the organization is heading.

4. A business needs to be ready to share what it takes to survive.

5. Operate under a "no surprises" policy

6. *Employees are the business, and nobody knows more about the business than they do!*

He continued, "would you care to take a stab at this one Sidney?"

"This one seems pretty easy too," started Sidney. "I would venture to say that Ricci was talking about exceptional communication."

"It's a little deeper than that though," interrupted Arthur. "We try to go beyond communication into something a little more meaningful. Sidney, what does communication contain?"

"When we communicate, we are passing information."

"And what does that information lead to?" coaxed Arthur.

"I would say that information leads to knowledge."

"By Jove, I think you've got it!" teased Arthur. "Communication passes on information which leads to knowledge. Now, what do you call it when we pass something on?"

Sidney thought for a second. "When we pass something on, we are transferring it."

"That's it Sidney!" jumped Arthur. "The 4th premise of the MOOSE is Knowledge Transfer. Since we are a MOOSE organization, we strive to do it better than anyone else, so the S would be..."

"Superior!" blurted Sidney.

"Exactly! The 4th premise of the MOOSE is Superior Knowledge Transfer!" he said excitedly.

Arthur, flushed with excitement, went to the notepad and wrote:

Superior Knowledge Transfer

Sidney, smiling, already had her hand out awaiting the piece of paper from Arthur. He handed it to her and she began to read.

Superior Knowledge Transfer

The moose excels at the transfer of information from moose to moose in the defending circle. What one moose learns from its surroundings, it unselfishly shares with the rest of the circle members. This information is shared between moose for the betterment of the circle. Knowing what to do in a harsh environment can mean the difference between life and death. The moose attempt to tip the balance of this situation in their favor by transferring how to survive to others.

To be a MOOSE organization, mechanisms must be in place to allow for a superior flow of knowledge within the organization. Everyone involved with the organization must know how the company is performing. What are the company's goals and objectives? Where is the company going? This philosophy must come from the top and be supported at all levels. From the administrative assistant, to accounting, to the hourly worker on the floor — all should be aware of the organization's status. No one person should hold all of the information for the organization.

A MOOSE organization should be a free information environment where employees are empowered in their decisions because they have the knowledge of the direction the organization is heading. To be a MOOSE organization, a business needs to be ready to share what it takes to survive! **A MOOSE knows that knowledge is power and transferring this power makes its circle stronger!**

"Arthur, this is exactly what Ricci was saying," Sidney said with excitement. "She explained to me the awesome job CatchAway has done in flowing information to everyone within the organization. On the tour, she showed me the work cells with all of the information posted. I understand now how important it is for everyone to be on the same page and know what goals and targets are in place. It seems to build enthusiasm in the employees as well. That was evident in the SOB meeting. All employees were enthused to present where they were in the business and how their department was helping the cause."

"That is brilliant, Sidney," complimented Arthur. "But be sure to understand that superior knowledge transfer needs to occur everywhere in the organization, not just on the plant floor. For this to work, information needs to be free flowing across all levels and all departments. All employees need to know the status of the business at all times."

Arthur went to the note pad and flipped to a blank sheet of paper. "So, Sidney, this is what we have so far." As Arthur spoke he wrote on the paper:

Motivating Organizational Development

Owned Hierarchy

Outrageous Customer Service

Superior Knowledge Transfer

"I guess that only leaves the E," remarked Sidney.

"Without the E, Sidney, the MOOSE is not complete," answered Arthur. "The E ties the rest of the MOOSE together into a neat package. It is all about why the business is here and what the business is striving to become. The E acts as a guide for all of our employees. Any ideas on what it could be, Sidney?"

Sidney paused for a second and then answered. "The only thing that we really haven't

talked about yet is what all businesses have — a
vision and mission. I don't see those being so
special because every business has one."

Arthur sat on the edge of his desk looking at
Sidney. Rubbing his chin, he began to speak.
"Those are very important to the MOOSE
Philosophy, Sidney. And, you are right, most
every business has a mission and a vision. It is
what most businesses DON'T *do* with these that
separate them from the MOOSE Philosophy.

"Most businesses have a mission/vision, and
that's it. The executives sit around and think up
things that sound great and look good on a wall.
If you ask the employees what the mission or
vision is, all you would get is a blank stare. We
believe the Mission, Vision, and Strategy of the
organization must be fully understood and lived
by all. This needs to be embraced by all to a point

where it is empowering enough to propel the business and its employees to greatness. And that's the 5th and final premise of the MOOSE — Empowering Mission, Vision, and Strategy. Here, I do have a written explanation for you."

"I knew you would," Sidney said with a smile.

Arthur handed her the piece of paper.

Empowering Mission, Vision, and Strategy

> A moose knows what its mission is in life — to survive. It also has a very keen sense of how it sees itself (its vision), and what it needs to do to survive (its strategy). The moose is "empowered" to make its own decisions. It knows that its actions are for the betterment of itself and its circle.

The mission, vision, and strategy in a MOOSE organization must mean something to its employees. It cannot be something that exists just for the sake of existing. For a MOOSE organization's employees to get something from the mission, vision, and strategy, the statements must be empowering. Every time the organization's employees see or hear the mission, vision, and strategy, they are urged, propelled, or motivated to act in the best interest of the business.

When well defined, communicated, and understood, the mission, vision, and strategy serve as a guide. This also provides a goal for all to strive and achieve for the betterment of the business.

If the MOOSE organization has done a

good job in defining itself, when an
employee is faced with a business decision,
they can effectively decide if it supports
what the business stands for. Thus, the
employee becomes empowered to make his
or her own sound decisions because he or
she understands what and how the decision
affects the business.
**A MOOSE knows what it needs to do to
survive!**

After a few minutes, Arthur began to speak.
"It is all about giving employees a goal, and
then getting out of the way. As long as all
employees know what it is we stand for and we
have competent people to carry out the plan, the
organization will thrive. Most businesses perform
in what I liken to a demolition derby."

"A demolition derby?" Sidney said with a puzzled look.

"Yes," Arthur said with a smile. "With an unclear mission, vision, or strategy, all of the employees are heading off in different directions. People are running into walls, other people, or simply spinning their wheels. The people are getting worn down, and the organization is going nowhere."

Sidney laughed as she began to speak. "I definitely get your point. Everyone in the organization needs to know the direction and why that direction has been chosen. People can then do their jobs, fully empowered, for the betterment of the business."

"I could not have said it better myself," said Arthur as he wrote the last MOOSE premise on the paper.

Motivating Organizational Development

Owned Hierarchy

Outrageous Customer Service

Superior Knowledge Transfer

Empowering Mission, Vision, and Strategy

Arthur continued, "Now, Sidney, you have the entire MOOSE! Philosophy. That's it. It all comes down to 'Choose the MOOSE!'. That is our mantra; our war cry. We invite people to 'Choose the MOOSE!' in everything they do. When they 'Choose the MOOSE!,' they are embracing the premises of what it means and what it takes to be the best they can be. A moose strives to be the best in order to survive. We need to 'Choose the

MOOSE!' in order to thrive!"

"Arthur," began Sidney, "this is incredible! I am so excited about the MOOSE! philosophy. I can't wait to finish my story on CatchAway. Everyone deserves to know about this philosophy and the great things it can accomplish."

"Yes, Sidney," stated Arthur. "It is a great philosophy, and it will accomplish great things, but, people need to realize it takes time and effort. It is not the management flavor-of-the-month, like so many organizations seem to come up with. It also is not something you do *to* people. It is something that is done with people over time for the betterment of themselves and the business. The MOOSE will accomplish great things if people just take the time to Choose It, Do It, and Live It! I look forward to seeing your article, Sidney. Please do not hesitate to contact me or anyone else in the CatchAway family. After all, we are here to serve!"

Arthur, with a warm smile, extended his hand to Sidney.

Sidney, in this short time, had developed a great respect for this man and his philosophy. At that moment, Alex rushed in to Arthur's office.

"Sorry to interrupt, Arthur," exclaimed Alex. "The folks from Australia are on the phone for you with quite an opportunity!"

Everyone said their professional goodbyes, and Sidney followed Alex out of Arthur's office. As she reached his doorway, she heard Arthur call out to her. "Sidney — Don't forget to Choose the MOOSE! in everything you do."

With a sparkle in her eye, Sidney responded, "Right back at ya!" as she high-fived Alex, smiled at Arthur, and continued out his door.

As Sidney made her way out of the CatchAway building, she ran into the janitor … literally. He was cleaning the glass door of the front entrance. In her excitement, she turned around to say "good bye" and "thank you" to the receptionist, and as he was coming in, she was going out and ended up plowing right into him! Her things flew everywhere.

"Oh my goodness! Are you okay?" Sidney quickly inquired with a face the shade of a tomato.

"Oh, I'm fine, ma'am. But, how are you?" he asked with a concerned look on his face.

"I'm just fine. I should have been watching where I was going," Sidney quickly admitted as they both stooped to collect her things.

"Say, do you have a minute?" she asked the man.

"Well, I do suppose I could spare a few, " answered the man." I reckon I'm runnin' a bit ahead of my work schedule. Now, what can I help you with little lady? By the way, my name's Ray. What might yours be?"

"My name's Sidney," she said as they shook hands.

She couldn't believe the size of Ray's hands. Her hand quickly became lost in his. But his shake was so gentle and friendly.

Sidney began, "How long have you worked here, Ray?"

"Well, I've been here for quite sometime now. I guess it's been about fifteen years or so. I picked up this job because I needed some extra money when my wife got sick."

"Oh. I'm sorry." Sidney replied.

"Not to worry. She's a tough woman and didn't let the illness get the best of her. Although sometimes I think puttin' up with me is a lot worse," he said with a big grin.

"I've seen a lot happen here over the years. My own personal views, this place is a whole lot better today than it was when I started. Once upon a time, us employees, we didn't get treated real well."

"Would you care to share that with me?" she asked.

"Well ma'am, why don't you first tell me what brings you here to CatchAway?"

"Oh, I'm sorry. I should have properly introduced myself at the start. I am a journalist working for *InFokus Magazine*. I've been interviewing several members of CatchAway's staff over the past few weeks. I was sent here to get information on why a moose is so important to this company."

"OK. I won't change my thoughts now that I know you could be quotin' me. I'll just speak the truth," began Ray. "Years ago, when I first came to CatchAway, I needed a job. The place didn't have the best name 'round town, but it's all I could find. I don't have but a grade school education, and the pickin's were slim.

"My wife needed treatments, and we needed money. So, I signed up. Come to find out, us people here at the lower end of the blue collar group didn't appear to exist much. We got bossed around and paid real poor like. Oh, there was some supervisors who wanted to help us out with training and more money but the boys at the top would hear nothin' of it. 'Doin' things for

employees costs money,' I heard 'em say once.
They were more about driving them fancy cars
and taking off for big trips to sunny places, if you
know what I mean."

"Were you given any opportunities at all?"
asked Sidney.

"Yeah. I could leave if I didn't like it,"
responded Ray. That's what I was told the day I
started. I felt real bad about that. I know'd I
wasn't qualified to do much else than sweep
floors and wash windows."

"But you're still here, fifteen years later,"
Sidney commented.

"I found a friend who helped me be someone
more than I was before," Ray answered. "Her
name is Ricci. She be runnin' the plant real well
all these years. She took a likin' to this old man
you're talkin' to. That kind lady took it upon

herself to get me some trainin' and somehow
more money too. I'm real grateful for her. Today,
I still sweep and clean windows. But I also do
maintenance jobs around this place and have even
taken some classes to learn more. She stuck with
it. And, a few years back, when we got ourselves
a new president, she had some words with him.
It was then we started to see things change, real
positive like."

"I've spoken with Ricci. She's quite a lady. I
don't think much gets by her," Sidney interjected
in an admiring tone about Ricci.

Ray continued, "Arthur, our president, really
turned things around for all us folks here. It's a
whole new place now. I don't mind coming to
work these days. That moose out front in the
grass greets us all before we walk in the door. It
means we all be real important. Who we are and

what we doin' matters to a lot of folks around here. Arthur and his folks care a whole lot about everybody, not just themselves.

"Ricci, she be working herself crazy to let them know how hard we all work and what our jobs mean to us. Since this moose wandered into our company, we be gettin' treated real well. We laugh and have a good time here. There's contests in the shop and prizes for reduced errors and rework. People be competin' for nobody gettin' hurt, and how long we all can go without missin' work."

"You sound very content and happy," stated Sidney.

"Ma'am," Ray answered, "this is the best job I ever had. I love what I be doin' and am workin' real hard at it you know? I be given the chance to make somethin' of myself. Arthur, he's a good man. I know we're lucky to have him be here. There ain't nobody else like him."

"Ray, I should probably let you get back to your job. I really appreciate your kind words. You've just summed up what all the others have had to say. What an incredible place to work. Enjoy the rest of your day, and thanks again!"

"Oh, you too, ma'am. I just be speaking from the heart you know? This is a good place full of a lot of good people. If I'm having a bad day, somebody always does something to make me smile. You take care now, and good luck with your article."

"Thank you Ray! Bye!"

"So long ma'am."

As she walked to her car, she couldn't help but smile. Her personal life before the MOOSE was completely without direction, and her professional life wasn't any better.

She found herself so energized; ready to tackle the world and present an awesome article for the public to read. Then she suddenly remembered how uninterested she was when William originally handed her the assignment. She remembered thinking to herself, "Great, a moose. What in the world am I supposed to do with an article about a moose?"

Now her thoughts ran wild. "What in the world would I do WITHOUT it? Leave it to a moose to straighten out my life!"

She shook her head and burst out in a fit of laughter as she began to drive back to the office. She now knew her life had a purpose. She was going to make something of herself and *InFokus*. Sidney had allowed the MOOSE! to show her the way!

Choose the MOOSE!

MOOSE Antlers
"Something to grow on"

Motivating Organizational Development

- A Moose knows what to do to properly grow within its environment.

- A Moose also knows that in order to keep thriving in its environment, it must adapt, change, and anticipant what changes are coming to its environment.

- A Moose knows where to look for food, where to find shelter, where to find its defending circle.

- A MOOSE! Organization must never underestimate a person's potential.

- A MOOSE! Organization must see that given the chance, anyone can accomplish something great.

- A MOOSE! Organization must know that people are its greatest assets, and it should do everything possible to develop those assets.

- A MOOSE! Organization should be building the people who are building the business.

Owned Hierarchy

- All of the moose in their defending circle know where they fit within the circle.

- When trouble arises, a moose knows where it can go for comfort, safety, and protection.

- Moose very rarely settle disagreements by fighting. The moose relies on its dominance, power, size and majesty within its circle of moose to determine the outcome of the disagreement.

- A MOOSE! Organization must allow its employees to know their "fit" in the organization.

- A MOOSE! Organization must know that by each employee understanding, knowing, and executing his or her own role, forward progress is unstoppable.

Outrageous Customer Service

- A moose knows what it needs to do outside of its circle to effectively serve others.

- A MOOSE! Organization must make serving others its number one priority.

- A MOOSE! organization must think of everyone as its customer and must strive to provide an outstanding experience to everyone time and time again.

- A MOOSE! Organization needs to be obsessed with providing its customers and consumers with outrageous customer service.

- A MOOSE! Organization needs to serve others and make each and every interaction a truly memorable one.

- A MOOSE! Organization needs to realize that the first time an issues arises, it is an opportunity. The second time the same issue arises, it is a problem.

Superior Knowledge Transfer

- What one moose learns from its surroundings, it unselfishly shares with the rest of its defending circle.

- Knowing what to do in the harsh environment means the difference between life and death to the moose.

- The moose attempt to tip the balance of a situation in their favor by transferring their "what" and "how" to survive to others.

- In a MOOSE! Organization the employees must know their ideas are welcomed and will be listened to.

- The MOOSE! Organization should be a free information environment where employees are empowered to make decisions because they have the knowledge of where the organization is heading.

- A MOOSE! Organization realizes that its employees are the business, and nobody knows more about the business than they do.

Empowering Mission, Vision, and Strategy

- A moose knows its mission in life—to survive.

- A moose has a keen sense of how it sees itself—its vision, and what it needs to do to survive—its strategy.

- The moose is "empowered" to make its own decisions because it knows that its actions are for the betterment of itself and of its circle.

- In a MOOSE! Organization, the well-defined, communicated, and understood mission, vision, and strategy serve as a guide.

- In a MOOSE! Organization, every time the organization's employees see or hear the mission, vision, and strategy, they are urged, propelled, and motivated to act in the best interest of the business.

About the Author

Peter A. Cicero, SPHR, MBA of Cicero Endeavors, Inc., has been in the "real" working world for more than 18 years. He draws from his vast experience as a chemist, operations director, general manager, and human resources professional to offer real solutions to organizational issues. Using his dynamic presenting ability, outstanding work experience, and his magnetic motivating personality, Peter facilitates workplace culture transformations. He has been transforming organizations for years by comparing life in the business world to that of life in nature. Using the moose as his motivation, Peter helps people transform themselves and their organizations into world famous entities!

He has been speaking professionally for seventeen years on topics including, but not limited to: *Culture in an Organization, Making Better Decisions to Achieve Personal and Organizational Goals, Teaching Companies to Think "Outside the Box," Creative Ways to Approach Problem Resolution* and *Choosing Your Attitude*. Peter can be e-mailed at pcicero@ciceroendeavors.com.

Cicero
Endeavors, Inc.

Cicero Endeavors specializes in guiding people to achieve outstanding attitudes and momentous energy.

Cicero Endeavors is changing the way people are approaching work and their lives.

Cicero Endeavors leads people on a journey to a better understanding of themselves, how they interact with others, and how they fit into the big picture.

We do not present a "canned" set of motivational tools that after a few days wear off. Nor do we teach any techniques that can seem forced, phony, or insincere. Your employees will journey with us to a better understanding of themselves, others, and the organization. Then, they will be able to form a synergistic team where negativity and politics are minimized in order to drive the business. They will begin a new life full of optimism, respect, and understanding.

Get started right with Cicero Endeavors!

Please give us a call at:
608-370-1411
or
608-370-1511

Our Website is:
www.ciceroendeavors.com

Services Available

Peter Cicero, through Cicero Endeavors, conducts incredible seminars and awesome consulting services in the areas of motivation, teamwork, vision/mission development, leadership, outrageous customer service, organizational development, personal development, and performance management.

Peter is available to make presentations and to conduct seminars. To make arrangements, please contact:

Cicero Endeavors, Inc.
608-370-1511

Visit us on our Web Site:
www.ciceroendeavors.com

Printed in the United States
64147LVS00003B/137